© 1993 Juliet & Charles Snape
by Julia MacRae Books
a division of Random House
20 Vauxhall Bridge Road
London SW1V 2SA

First published 1993

This 1995 edition published by
Derrydale Books, distributed by
Random House Value Publishing,
40 Englehard Avenue,
Avenel, NJ 07001

Random House
New York • Toronto • London • Sydney • Auckland
A CIP catalog record for this book is available
from the Library of Congress

MY BOOK OF PICTURE
PUZZLES

JULIET AND CHARLES SNAPE

Derrydale Books
New York • Avenel

Party puzzles

Follow the streamers to find which present is in which box.

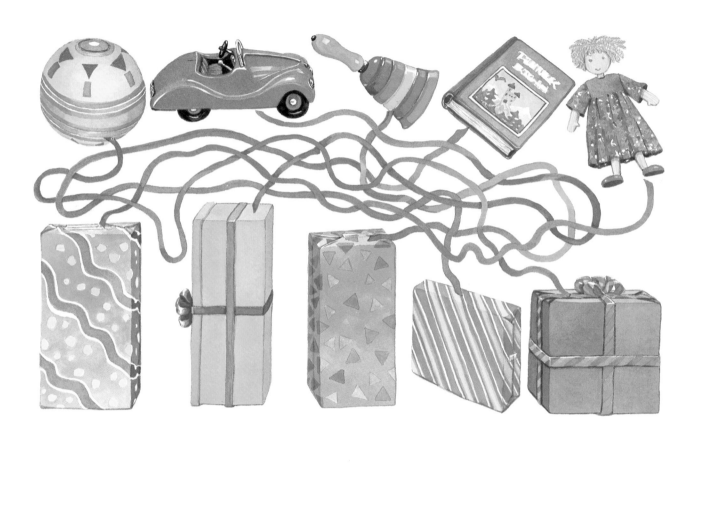

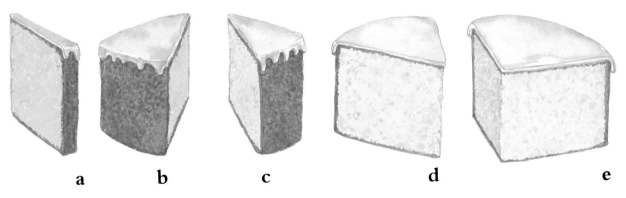

a   b   c   d   e

These five slices have been cut out from the cakes on the table in the picture on the opposite page. Can you match the slices to the cakes?

Five friends are hiding in the picture. Can you spot them?

Rabbit's problem

Fox is waiting for little Rabbit to come out.
Can you find the way through the burrows
that will take Rabbit to the only safe way out?

Reflections

Which mirror shows Teddy's correct reflection?
Try putting your teddy bear in front of a mirror.

Can you work out the reflections for each letter in the mirrors?
Which ones look the same in the mirror as outside?

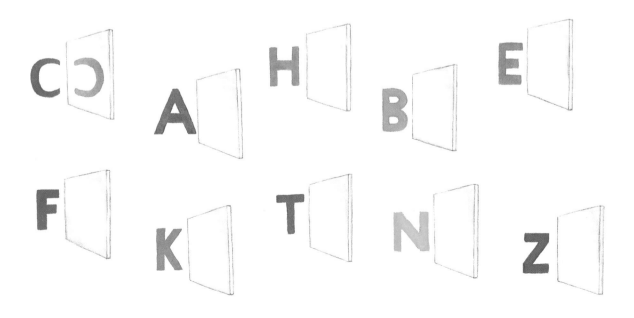

The strange lake

Can you see what is wrong with the reflections in the lake?
(There are eight things to spot.)

The ghostly puzzle

The little ghost has lost its shadow. Which one is it?

How many witch's brooms can you spot?
How many hidden faces can you find?

In the garden

Can you find the largest bee?
She lives in the hive that has two front legs,
a round hole, and a yellow roof. Which one is it?

There are lots of socks on the clothesline, but there are
only two that match. Can you find the pair?
What is funny about the apple trees?

Holiday snaps

a

b

c

d

Can you put these holiday photos in the order
in which they were taken?

Which things go together?

Can you sort these things into four groups,
each with three objects?

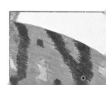

Island bridges

Can you walk around the islands crossing every bridge only once?
Start on any island. You may visit an island more than once and
you don't have to finish on the island where you started.

Which island do you think the treasure map is for?

Story muddles

The picnic

1

2

3

4

The see-saw

1

2

3

4

Can you put these stories in the right order?

Match the hat

Which hat fits into which box?

Jigsaw pieces

Can you work out where the six jigsaw pieces belong?

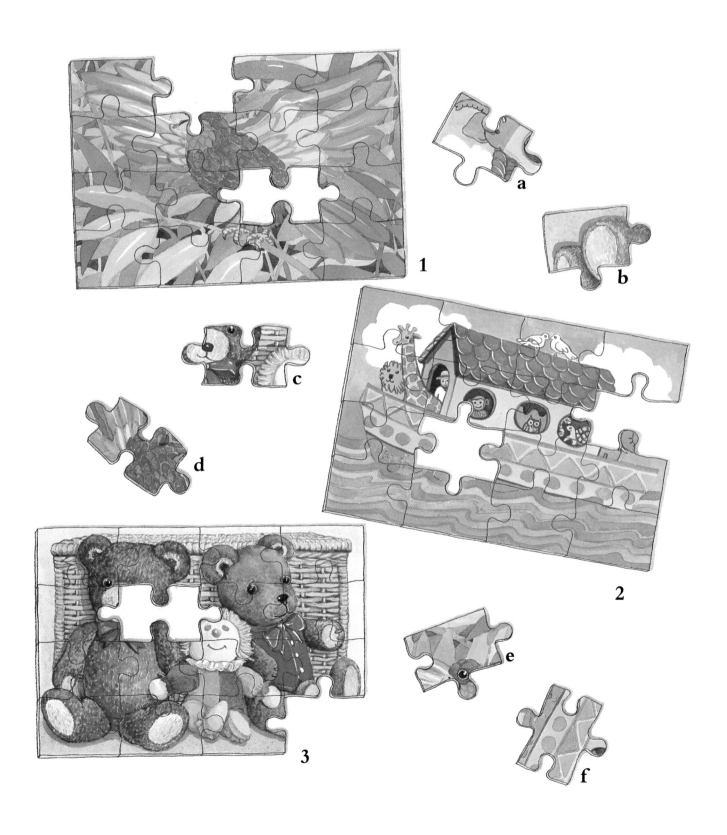

The odd room

There are lots of very odd things about
this room. How many can you find?

Odd one out

Can you find the odd one out in each of these sets?

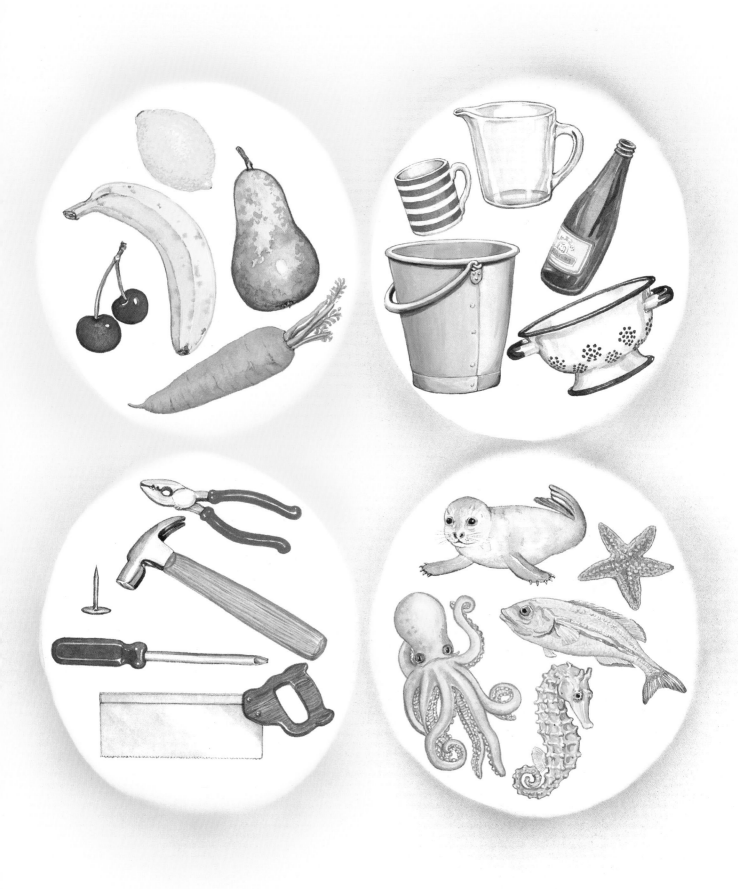

At the top

Entrance

There's a long cool drink waiting on
the roof garden. Can you find a route
through the building from the entrance?

Funny people

Can you decide which pieces below belong to which funny person?
It might help to trace the figures and draw in the missing parts.

Can you make a funny person for yourself
using only circles, squares or triangles?

Puzzle Cat

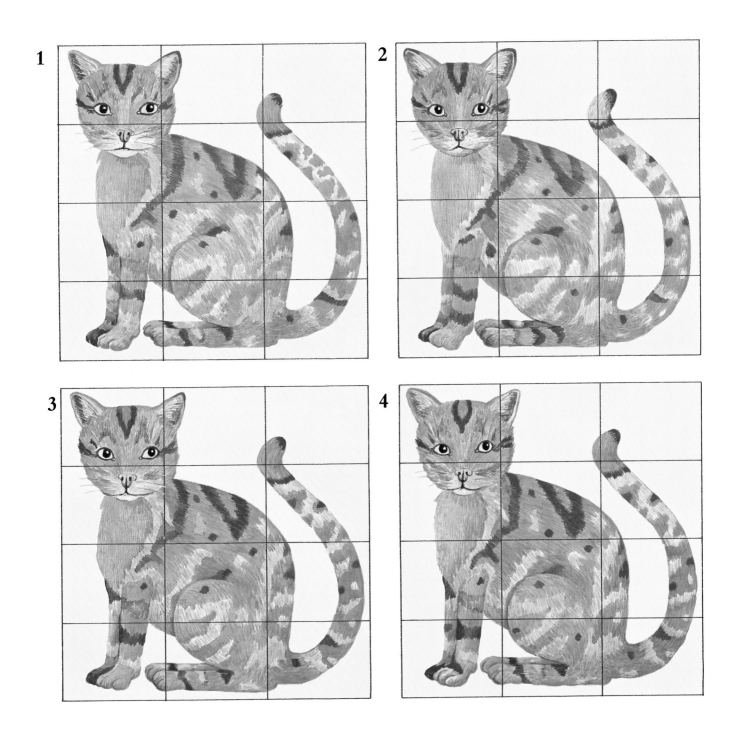

Hidden on each lower right-hand corner of this
book is a piece of a Puzzle Cat. Which one of the cats
above is the completed Puzzle Cat?

Answers

Party puzzles
Slice **a** belongs to cake **4**.
Slice **b** belongs to cake **2**.
Slice **c** belongs to cake **1**.
Slice **d** belongs to cake **5**.
Slice **e** belongs to cake **3**.

Rabbit's problem

Reflections
Teddy's reflection on the left is the correct one.
A, H and T stay the same. Can you think of any other letters that stay the same? What happens when you put the mirror underneath the letters?

The strange lake
In the reflection you will find: a round bridge instead of a straight one; two children instead of one; a moon on a sunny day; two pink extra bulrushes; a different tree; the frog missing; the duck back to front; an owl instead of a blackbird.

The ghostly puzzle
Shadow number 4 is the ghost shadow.

There are seven hidden faces and seven witch's brooms.

In the garden
The matching socks are on the far left and third from the right.

Holiday photos
The order is **d b a c.**

Which things go together?
Goldfish, bowl and pondweed.
Deckchair, flip-flop and sunglasses.
Knife, fork and plate.
Trowel, seeds and watering can.

Island bridges

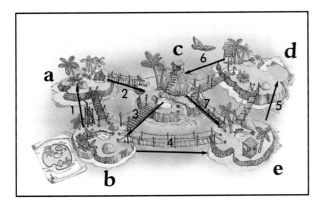

If you start on island **b** you can cross the seven bridges once only by following the arrows in the order marked. Can you work out a route if you start on island **e**?
Island **e** is the one shown in the treasure map.

Story muddles
The picnic: **4 1 3 2**
The see-saw: **3 1 4 2**

Match the hat
1 e 2 c 3 a 4 b 5 d

Jigsaw pieces
Pieces **d** and **e** belong to **1**.
Pieces **f** and **a** belong to **2**.
Pieces **b** and **c** belong to **3**.

The odd room

There are at least twenty things to spot.

Odd one out
We chose: the carrot (the only vegetable); the colander (the only one that cannot hold water); the nail (the others are tools); the seal, (the only mammal). Can you think of other answers that are also true?

Puzzle Cat
Puzzle Cat is cat number 4. You could make a Puzzle Cat jigsaw by cutting out all the corner pieces hidden in the book. This won't spoil any other puzzles.

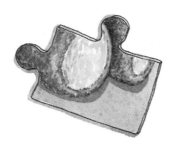